OBSERVED

Art must be for woman like a personified ancient ritual
where every spiritual thought is made visible, enacted, represented.
Art must be like a miracle . . . art is a miracle.

Anaïs Nin

OBSERVED:

*From a Film Portrait of
a Woman as Artist*

by Robert Snyder

THE SWALLOW PRESS INC.
CHICAGO

12/1977
Am. Lit.

Additional Credits:
Photographs on pages 33-35, 41, 56, 68, 74, 97, 101 are reproduced by permission of Harcourt Brace Jovanovich, Inc., from *A Photographic Supplement to the Diary of Anais Nin*, copyright © by Anaïs Nin.

Photographs on pages 60 and 61 of Martha Graham and her dance group are reproduced by permission of Barbara Morgan from her book *Martha Graham: Sixteen Dances in Photographs*, Duell, Sloan and Pierce (New York, N.Y.: 1941). The closeup of Miss Graham is reproduced from the film *A Dancer's World* produced by Nathan Kroll.

Extracts from Henry Miller's Paris notebooks and letters are used with the kind permission of the author: letter to William A. Bradley, August 2, 1933, first published in *Max and the White Phagocytes* (Obélisque Press, Paris: 1938); and "Un Être Etoilique," first published in *Sunday After the War* (Editions Poetry, London: 1945); the Paris notebooks are unpublished.

The Swallow Press, Incorporated
811 West Junior Terrace
Chicago, Illinois 60613

Printed in the United States of America

Library of Congress Catalog Card Number 76-3123

International Standard Book Number 0-8040-0708-x

For my darling daughter Alexandra, in the hope that,
she too, will achieve self-realization and serenity.

ACKNOWLEDGMENTS

I am especially grateful to Rupert Pole above all the many who assisted me in making this finished book—as, indeed, the film *Anais Nin Observed* from which the book is derived—an actuality. His loving devotion to Anaïs and his knowledge of her work and the vast archives of extant pictures, mss., and texts eased the burden on Anaïs and made my job smoother.

My heartfelt thanks to my "team" of editor—Ruth Glushanok—and art director—Kadi Tint, whose combined knowledge of the author, the craft of bookmaking, taste, and critical judgment helped me fashion this book.

We were all privileged to work with Donna Ippolito, Miss Nin's editor at Swallow Press, for additional material, especially from the author's fiction, and for the suggestions that considerably enriched the book; and John Ferrone, Miss Nin's editor at Harcourt Brace Jovanovich, Inc., for materials from the *Diaries* and the *Photographic Supplement* which they published.

The credit for all the photographs enlarged from the film negative goes to Baylis Glascock, director of photography on the film; for the production stills credit is again due to Baylis Glascock, and for production portraits of Ms. Nin, to our film editor Robert A. Fitzgerald, Jr. We had additional assistance from Jaime Snyder in photo selection and preparation, and from Ms. Nin's own extensive collection of photographs where Rupert Pole, of course simplified our task.

I take this occasion to thank again the sources for film and photo quotations as listed in the film's program notes (page viii), and for the portraits of Harry Partch, thanks to Betty Freeman; for the classic dance photos of Martha Graham used with her kind permission and with the permission of Barbara Morgan from her book *Martha Graham: Sixteen Dances in Photographs*.

My special thanks to Wernher Krutsin/Dymaxion Photographs for lab preparation of the photos. And once again to Brooke Whiting, curator of rare books, Department of Special Collections, Research Library, UCLA.

PROGRAM NOTE

Anaïs OBSERVED: *A Film Portrait of a Woman as Artist*
by Robert Snyder

<u>Anais Nin talks with, and about:</u>

Dr. Otto Rank

Antonin Artaud

D. H. Lawrence

Lawrence Durrell

Henry Miller   (from Robert Snyder's THE HENRY MILLER ODYSSEY)

Edmund Wilson

Frances Steloff   (at the Gotham Book Mart; photographed by Arnold Eagle)

Maya Deren   (from her RITUAL IN TRANSFIGURED TIME—Grove Press Films)

Isamu Noguchi   (from Arnold Eagle's NOGUCHI: A Sculptor's World)

Martha Graham   (from Barbara Morgan's photographs; and Nathan Kroll's A DANCER S WORLD)

Lloyd Wright   (at his Wayfarer's Chapel, Portuguese Bend, Calif., for the Swedenborgian Society)

Harry Partch   (from KPBS-TV's THE MUSIC OF HARRY PARTCH)

Renata Druks   (collages)

Kenneth Anger   (from his INAUGURATION OF THE PLEASURE DOME—Film Maker's Cooperative, N.Y.)

Jean Varda   (from THE HENRY MILLER ODYSSEY)

Quartet   (violins - Dennis Townsend, Norma Wilson
viola - Rupert Pole; cello - Harriet Berman
playing excerpts from The Brahms B-flat String Quartet, Opus 67)

Lou Andreas-Salomé

Caresse Crosby   (from Robert Snyder's "ALWAYS YES," CARESSE and Emlen Etting's POEM 8)

A group of young women writers from UCLA

John Green and dancers at the Cumberland Mountain Film Studio, Venice

Tom Schiller

     *   *   *   *   *   *   *   *   *   *

Director of Photography .... Baylis Glascock
Editors .... R. A. Fitzgerald, Jr.; Tom Schiller
Sound Recordists .... John Glascock; Leslie Shatz
Re-recording .... George Porter, Ryder Sound Services, Inc.
Associate Director .... R. A. Fitzgerald, Jr.
Production Assistants .... Gilbert Jaffe; Nick James; Diana Murphy
Color by DeLuxe

— made possible in part with a grant from the Judith S. Thomas Foundation —

copyright, 1973, by

MASTERS & MASTERWORKS *PRODUCTIONS, INC.*   *6363 Wilshire Boulevard, Suite 218, Los Angeles, California 90048*

PREFACE

> *. . . the exultant message of American Democracy, of souls on the Open Road, full of glad recognition, full of fierce readiness, full of joy of worship when one soul sees a greater soul—the only riches, the great souls.*

D. H. Lawrence thus concludes his essay on Walt Whitman in *Studies in American Literature.* Seeing greater souls has been my life's passion, imagining myself first in my adolescent dream life to be, or at least to encounter, a Bach, a Mozart, John Milton, Martha Graham, Fred Astaire, Michelangelo—add your own hero or heroine to the roster; the list is without end. And then, wish to thought to deed, it has dominated my working life as well, being drawn to artists, musicians, writers, dancers—antennae of the race if not makers of its civilization.

How did I get that way?

Inhibitions against sensory experience start early in life: Don't. Don't feed the animals, don't walk on the grass, don't touch the object, and surely not the person. As a helpless nonadult, a child either accedes or rebels, but grows, grows up, in spite of prohibitions: by hook or by crook. I grew up, more or less, overreacting against rules and regulations imposed by any authority, however well-meaning, however necessary the rules might have seemed to be—might, in fact, to this day seem to be. Clearly, such prohibitions, whether against touching the glass vase or smoking pot or reading pornographic novels or whatever, only heighten curiosity and, at their best, encourage further experimentation.

In fact, there are many alternatives: splitting to the open road, petty thievery, eavesdropping, rape, voyeurism, and perhaps the worst of all, resignation . . . or sublimation of one's cravings into artifacts. It was, I believe fortunately, the last that called to me most insistently. The more numerous the impediments, the greedier a consumer of the arts did I become; all the more did I yearn to possess, to know by direct perception. It was through film that I was able to experience, not only the work, but its source, the creator of the work, warts and all. For film is a medium that leaps across vast distances, through time and space and the stoutest walls into the presence of the masters and their masterworks. It is a virtual museum and concert hall and theater, unencumbered by ceilings and walls, the next best thing to the thing itself.

For me, these films are voyages of discovery. They start from an innocent craving to experience the subject as closely as possible and from a smattering of ignorance. If I were an expert on Michelangelo like, say, de Tolnay, or on de Kooning like, say, Harold Rosenberg, I wouldn't make a film. If anything, I'd write a book which might add some information about the subject, whereas my documentary film voyage is, at best, an experience *of* the subject.

But I am not a film freak and I cannot even pretend to believe that film is the be-all and the end-all of the arts. Nonetheless, each of the media, each of the arts, has its own quiddity, its own essential nature. Nor are they recklessly translatable one into the other. A film is a film, a book is a book, a symphony, a symphony—just as surely as a rose is a rose is a rose.

What am I to do then, when I have completed a film and am still not an expert in any sense on the subject with whom I have been so deeply involved during its making, yet I find myself in possession of a great deal of source material from sound track—monologues, dialogues, conversations, and from film—the twenty-four photo images per second which alone are capable of projecting that intimate actuality peculiar to the art of photography. What the tiny frames may lack in "art"-photo quality in book form, is more than counterbalanced by the sense of live action they convey.

Such materials offer another dimension to the full realization of the subject, the "next best thing" to the film itself, the "next best thing" to the living presence of the creator and his work. Considering the present popularity of picture books for adults, I began to urge this upon the publishers: *not* a coffee-table book, for God's sake, but a respectable piece of work, made easily available for an interested audience, inexpensively, and without barriers—especially without the barriers of experts. I am constantly at odds with my editor arguing that the text is not literature, nor are the photographs art, but must, like the film, complement each other to open up and reveal a personality or a subject.

Do you remember the scene in *Citizen Kane* when the researcher is admitted into a steel-vault chamber just to look at a document under the minute and careful scrutiny of an armed guard? There was something sinister about it in the movie; in reality it is rather ridiculous that it should take special letters of introduction to get into the archives that bureaucratically separate the artist from his audience. I managed, in the course of my work, to penetrate the Henry Miller archives in the special collection at UCLA's Powell Library and the Gertrude Stein collection at Yale with the utmost difficulty. No one could call this accessibility! As we go to press I hear that Anaïs Nin's papers have been acquired by the UCLA library. . . .

If Gutenberg's invention of movable type put the Bible into the hands of everyman and precipitated the Reformation, modern printing technology could take the arts and letters now restricted to the shelves of special libraries and the homes of the wealthy and place them in the hands of students, if not in the hands of the masses, and cause a minor Renaissance. Why not?

A publisher finally accepted the manuscript of a prospective book to be made from my film, *The Henry Miller Odyssey*. It was no picnic, and not even precisely what I had visualized, but last year saw the publication of *This Is Henry, Henry Miller from Brooklyn*. Although I thrashed about uncomfortably throughout the making of the book, I now admit to being quite proud of it. In its fresh encounter with Miller the film removed many of the hard-of-access library shelf materials from their vaults, and placed them out there, in full and plain view of any interested passerby. The book took the new resources of text and picture and unused mss, memorabilia, facsimiles, and extracts from books and letters, and put it out at only $5.95 a copy.

It wasn't a best seller any more than the film was a blockbuster, but the response was healthy; popular scholarship continues to plug away through the years, and signaled the desirability of putting together similar books based on films. Swallow Press, the publisher of Anaïs Nin's novels, asked me to put together a book based on my film, *Anais Observed*.

So here is Anaïs.

ROBERT SNYDER
SUMMER 1976

Anaïs Nin
OBSERVED

My feet were treading paper and a stairway of ivory piano notes.
These were the streets of my own diary, crossed with bars of black notes.
I was lost in the labyrinth of my confessions
among the veiled faces of my acts. . . .
I heard the evening prayer, the cry of solitude recurring every night . . .
Enormous rusty keys opened each volume,
and the figures passed and vanished, armless or headless,
multilated, as I had unburied them.
The white orifice of the endless cave opened.
On the rim of it stood a little girl eleven years old
carrying the diary in a little basket.

*Someone asked me to pronounce
my first name — — —*

three times (Laughter and applause.) I must do that—it's
very important—because five little girls have been named after me. So you
have to learn the name: it's Ahna-ees, Ahna-ees, Ahna-ees; like Anna with
ees added onto it. This is to the future Anaïs's." That was in the waiting
period after a lecture and reading that closed the Anaïs Nin weekend furrawn at UC Berkeley.

"Mythologize her," Henry Miller enjoined me when I started my film portrait of Anaïs.

To be sure, the ingredients for a myth were immediately apparent. I first met her at the Ash Grove, one of the few cafés in Los Angeles, an underground night-club for jazz freaks, fans of folk singing, poetry readings, films. I had been invited there to show my film of Caresse Crosby, and while making the customary introduction and scanning the intime assembly before me, one face stood out from the mist of faces that make up an audience.

The screening was followed, as was customary, by discussion and comment. It was then that the apparition materialized. Anaïs Nin identified herself matter-of-factly, and in a fragile but firm voice she made the most clear-cut and generous remarks about by work. It was not until some time later that I discovered she knew Caresse and had herself written an insightful portrait of the lady.

So this was Anaïs Nin: beautiful, delicately alluring, gentle, but unpretentious and with a tensile strength of mind and character; and most graciously generous—but not inviting me into her privacy—mysterious. All the ingredients of a Muse. And having entered my life from the shadows, she faded back out.

I did not meet her again until 1968, a few years later, when I was filming Henry Miller. In their encounter in the Paris of the 1930s, Henry had nourished and been nourished by her presence—as their published correspondence well documents. But more, he had an important and early role in fashioning her legend. Recalling his Paris years in The Henry Miller Odyssey, my film portrait of him, Miller spoke freely about Anaïs's place in those picaresque years:

> Here I make the best friends of my life. I had two especially boon companions, Lawrence Durrell and Alfred Perlès. And, of course, there was a third person, perhaps more important than either of them, and that was Anaïs Nin, author of the now famous diaries, an inspiration to and protectress of so many striving artists—including yours truly.

In one of their letter exchanges on The Tropic of Cancer, he addressed her as "madame la sorcière, femme de lettres, charmeuse":

4

Madame ANAIS NIN femme de lettres

sorcière

charmeuse

reçoit

à Louveciennes

Anais' Notes on Trop. of Cancer.

The man so humiliated and buffeted by the world
imprisoned in nightmare of self-assertion, challenging the passerby with his bitterness, imposing
on the whole world a share in his delirium and
self-laceration, performing before the world the
double horror of flagellating himself and then
turning madly to whip the blood out of the watchers
It is the frenzy of a man with so terrifying a ven-
genance that the cause of the vengeance is lost
sight of. It has become trivial. Here is a man
who because he has starved, stolen, begged, de-
dceived, loved, worked at humiliating tasks, hits
back with art, an art so belligerent, murderous
riotous and fecund that the injury he has received no one would want to wipe from the world. The
world as a spectator is poisoned and ~~thronwed~~ prodded
out of its inertia, it is led into the orgy of
insults and fury, it is tormented and dissolved--
but it knows, through the drama, that the monstrous
devoration of reality is reaching its climax in exp
pression; it realizes that a climax is an end in
itself, that if injured and injurious can meet in
a dance of madness it has lived through an hour
of such acuity of vision, as it will never again
possess, for here is the groaning image of the
greatest bitterness in the world, the greatest
loneliness, the most horrible defeat, the most
criminal upheaval, the sight of the operation
of the world's worst cancers and leprosy-- an
exposed world, splintered open, holding no more
secret pain and therefore no more fear. The
monsters are made to appear but they are attacked.
H. M. attacks them for us, calls them by their
immonde names, recreates the most realistic cruci-
fication ever created--man crucifying himself to
show only the torments of the imagination, the
awful power of self-created sorrows, of a violence
unequalled, unanswerable by the gods--the man
crucified by knowledge of the world and the
dreams and nightmares which follow it--or precede

Henry suggested that it would be a fine thing to film a session with Anaïs; and, indeed, it was. One session led to another, in the course of which we became friendly, potentially friends.

One of the lesser benefits of being admitted to her charmed circle, I soon found out, was that you get on her mailing list. Periodically, I would receive a postcard calling attention to some event or other, generally avant-garde, experimental, off-Broadway, underground, counterculture. I think Anaïs realized early, like Gertrude Stein before her, that the "secret of my success is my small audience."

And so one day a postcard from her arrived announcing the opening of a new art gallery in that architectural jewel of deteriorating downtown Los Angeles, the Bradbury Building, with a show of the work of Varda, the collagist whose brilliant pieces I had come to admire in Henry's house.

Henry was going, of course; and, of course, he thought it would be fine to film a session for his Odyssey *at the show—and we did. I watched Anaïs there, as, resplendent, she ascended the tortuous baroque staircase. Laughing, I remarked to her what a beautiful little surrealist art short could be made by simply filming her, slow motion, through the open stairwell as she walked up the steps and floated along and around each balustraded landing, up and around, and on out through the vaulted glass roof.*

It was the first hint, even if half in jest, that I would film her. She laughed her musical laugh.

Anaïs generously, as always, helped me over my toughest hurdles in completing my film of Henry, spurring me on to persist, despite its difficulties, by inscribing my copies of volume one of the Diary, *"For Bob, . . . Your friend," and volume two, "For Bob with love."*

For Bob –
...sh you had
...een there with
... camera!

Yours friend
Anaïs

For Bob –
for the enjoyment
of your Miller Odyssey
your gift for
portraying others

Affectionately
Anaïs

For Bob
equally engaged in
portraits of our intimate
a skilful and
human portrayal
in films

with love
Anaïs

In December 1969, after a successful launching of The Henry Miller Odyssey *on the West Coast and a screening by invitation at the Edinburgh Film Festival, the* Harvard Advocate *requested a benefit of an East Coast premiere in association with the International Association for Cultural Freedom. I was invited to come, and, of course, they prayed that the star himself would attend. Alas, Henry would make no personal appearances, but by a stroke of luck Anaïs was in the East for the publication of* Diary III. *The* Advocate *urged that if the film's "star" would not make a personal appearance, perhaps its principle "featured player" would share the stage with me. Happily, she would and did.*

Our vaudeville turn proved to be good fun, and I joked that we should go on the circuit together. Marian Schlesinger gave her a full-page feature interview in the Boston Daily Globe, *commenting that judging from the audience response to her presence, Robert Snyder might be well-advised to film the odyssey of Anaïs Nin.*

Hmmm. This was not the first time I had been privately pondering this attractive idea. But, I reminded myself, I'm not into her work—remembering almost simultaneously that when I started the Miller project I was not much more into his either. In fact, something Henry said in the film seemed to make it all possible. "You'd think," he said, "that an author has definite plans and ideas and all that; well, he does in a slight way. But you write in order to find out what you're writing about, who you are and why and what for. It's a voyage of discovery. . . . *The object is not to know where you're going."*

A voyage of discovery beckoned. Back in Los Angeles I broached the subject to Anaïs.

Well, why not?

For starters, there was the ever pernicious lack of obtainable funds to back a documentary. Then, her shyness, her timidity, and the matter of invading her private life. And, also, that female vanity: "You know, I'm not an ingenue any more." She was reassured on all levels by the knowledge that Baylis Glascock, who had photographed her for the Miller film, would be director of photography.

Baylis agreed that the aura of mystery that surrounds her could best be served through soft focus—sfumato—by reflets dans l'eau, dans verres, *and would use appropriate filters.*

Moreover, she knew I would make a film of *her, rather than* about *her. A film might even serve as a substitute for her live presence and meet the growing demands of colleges and other institutions for lectures, seminars, and an altogether impossible schedule of one-night stands. When Judith Stark, of Los Angeles's Theatre Vanguard made us an initial grant, we were propelled into it. I was on my way to a new voyage of discovery.*

We arrived with a modest amount of equipment and an immodest amount of brass to flesh out a myth in twenty-four frames per second—a film portrait of a woman as artist. It was a very gray day, and we bewailed the lack of natural light when suddenly, as occasionally happens in Los Angeles, the clouds precipitated into rain. Knowing the shower would be short-lived, we moved hurriedly to the edge of her little pool, and, equipment, crew, and star protected by the overhanging eaves of the house, I knelt down and whispered, "How and where did it all begin?"

*I don't know how far
my memory wants to go today.*

But the water makes me think of my first break with my roots:
taking the ship from Spain to America, which is when the diaries began.
That was my first journey; a journey which was also a bridge.
A breaking of a bridge with Europe, and with my father. . . .
I don't know but it must have been since that time that I kept the love of water
as the most important element of my life.
The idea of travel . . . perhaps the idea of returning to Europe.
Because I associated all travel with ships,
I have a great love of ships, a great love of journeys.
So I'd say it began with a voyage,
which was a loss and a breaking away from one continent
to go to another continent.

It started on that ship, which represented
a very threatening journey to an unknown land . . .
to tell the story of the journey.

The diary didn't begin as a diary; it began as a letter to my father. So I was very careful to note every detail of life on board the ship—at that time it took thirteen days to come from Spain—and every detail of the arrival.

Then I made special entries describing this new country, perhaps to entice him to come. He didn't know any English, and so it was all very foreign to him. It may have been my mother's wish to take us into another culture to which he could not follow.

As far back as I can remember I began what became a lifelong practice of daily recording the real in a journal, as sketches for writing the unreal. Some of the early entries are religious. I was very much into the Catholic mysteries as a child. I dreamed of Saint Joan; I hoped to become Saint Anaïs.

14

Pardon mes chers petits
Arias Thorwald et je veux
avec toute ma pensée
J. Nin
Paris 1916 MCMXVI

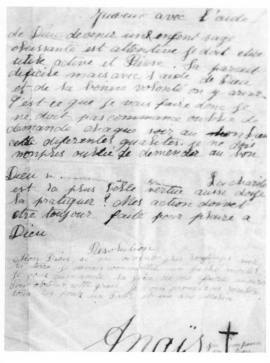

Voilà mon Papa, mon chère Papa.

Recuerdo cariñoso à la señora
Isidra Sang de

15

My little basket in which
I carried my diary when I came from Spain to America
—I never let go of that little basket.

16

WE ARE GOING TO NEW YORK

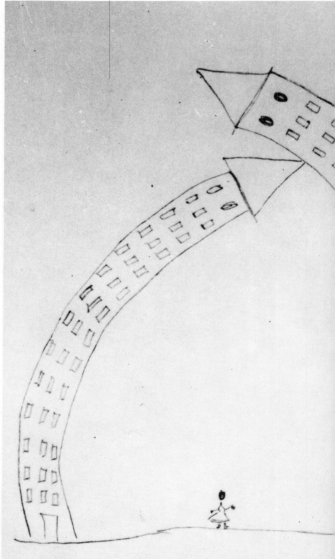

IN NEW YORK YOU CANNOT SEE

I made up picture stories at the age of eleven: my image of what America was to be like—peopled by Indians with tents and feathers.

Instead I found the very tall buildings of New York that made it impossible to see the sky.

School seemed like a prison; and I depicted the school window
as a prison window—
all the feelings that children have!

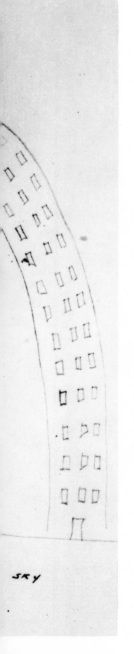

Yes, I guess the whole thing, the letters, descriptions, and drawings
were for my father.

Then my mother said I couldn't mail them because they might get lost.
In that way she really made me keep them
though they weren't intended to be a diary.

It started as a letter to my father and ended as a letter to the world.
And now it's a correspondence—a communion with the whole world.

20

Élan!

Maman chéri, ô! je t'aime. je t'aime
je ne saurais que faire pour toi demande!
demande! je le ferais

Anaïs

Maman
chanteuse
délicieuse
Maman
tendre mère
aimante
Maman
mère dévou
a ses enfants

Anaïs

Maman
mérite plus
que le ciel,
Dieu dois
avoir un
ciel pour
une maman
comme ma
maman
mais ce ciel
ne seras que
pour elle et
car personne
qu'elles ne le
mérite

Anaïs

Mme Rosa C. Nin
Chanteuse
et
Mère tendre et aimante

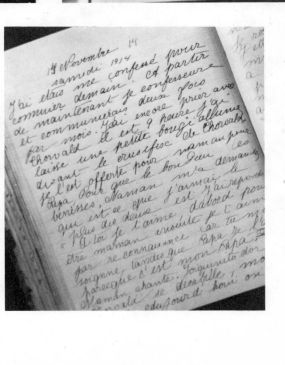

21

I accumulated so many volumes that I finally lost coun

—and put them in a bank vault in Brooklyn.

It was in the sixties, I think, when I began to realize that the characters I had described in the diary had a dynamic influence on the present—Henry Miller, Larry Durrell, Antonin Artaud. Also, I felt that my novels were not understood, and had created a wall between myself and the world. Being a person obsessed with relationships, I suffered very much from that wall.

I found out very early that neurosis interferes with creation; that an artist creates in spite of neurosis. You've seen many writers who write just one theme all their lives. I think that without psychoanalysis, I could have written, all my life, the story of a daughter's quest for her father, whereas each moment of evolution in psychoanalysis really helped me get into another cycle. I don't mean that we get rid of, completely rid of, painful or sorrowful experiences, but that you don't remain fixed and obsessed with just one experience.

And this flow I owe to psychoanalysis. In fact, I owe everything to it: the stability, the confidence in myself (of which I had absolutely none), the ability to talk with the world—all those things which I do not possess naturally, or which were interfered with by neuroses—appeared when the neurosis vanished.

And my writing suddenly tapped a source which is absolutely endless and infinite. There is no end to the free association of ideas and images and themes and discoveries opening up—of mysteries—all this I think I owe to psychoanalysis.

24

I always tell young writers that I can't imagine anything more wonderful for them than to have either a love affair or analysis—because they put you in touch with your creativity—and creativity comes from the subconscious. I advise young writers to keep diaries as a discipline. Writing every day, as one practices the piano every day, keeps one nimble, and then, when the great moments of inspiration come, one is in good form, supple and smooth.

The diary deals always with the immediate present,
the warm, the near,
being written at white heat develops a love of the living moment.
One thing is very clear—
that both diary and fiction tend towards the same goal:
intimate contact with people, with experiences, with life itself.

Well, we've started; and not a bad trajectory at that. Our next session interrupts her at work—and it is a very demanding schedule she follows. Yet, she cooperates spontaneously, unaffectedly, as though we were her guests.

I remarked politely on the charm of her colorful dress, a compliment she brushed aside with a delighted laugh; just something she picked up in a thrift shop. Lunchtime? She sweeps regally into the kitchen, floats through it picking up an elegant lunch—salad, cheese, cold cuts, fruit, tea, wine—and sets it out like a flower arrangement. So it goes, pleasantly, almost effortlessly.

The only problem, and it is small indeed, is Piccolino, her white toy poodle, who's always underfoot, cavorting into a scene and staring into the camera demandingly. I hear myself sternly, but under my breath, commanding—as I always had to do to passersby when shooting on location in Italy—"Non guardare in macchina!" Don't look into the camera. The whole thing was rather like a party instead of a filming.

She's working on the diaries and we get into the question of why she published them when they were not written with publication in mind; the principal influences in her life; her cultural landscape.

And the film goes that route as well, back from the present to her past life and forward again into the present.

28

*When I was
working on the diary I became
aware of a wonderful image;*
relationships were very much like stellar constellations—friendships gravitated around the cities of my life, Paris, New York, Los Angeles . . .

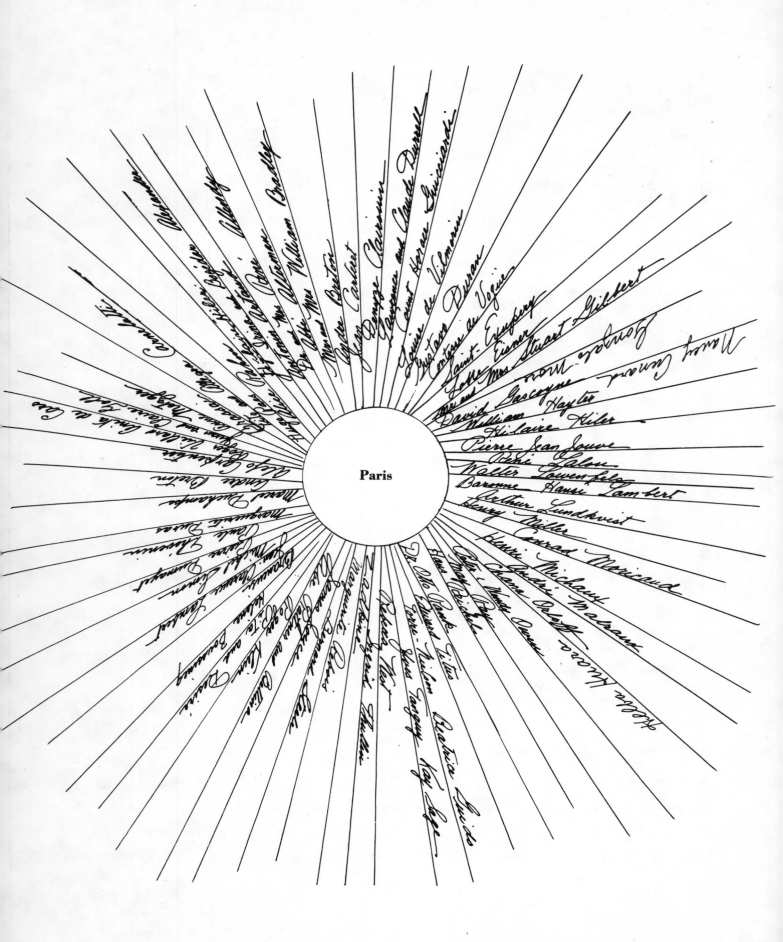

In Paris

Henry Miller—when Henry appeared, what was so obvious about him was his tremendous joy in life, his enjoyment of everything, his curiosity about everything.

She speaks of herself mockingly at times as "une étoilique"—a word which she has invented, and why not, since, as she says, we have the word *lunatique*; why not "étoilique?"

Hers is the first female writing I have ever seen: it rearranges the world in terms of female honesty. The result is a language which is ultra-modern and yet which bears no resemblance to any of the masculine experimental processes with which we are familiar. It is precise, abstract, cloudy and unseizable. . . . There is not an ounce of man-made culture in it, everything related to the head is cut off. Time passes, but it is not clock time; nor is it poetic time such as men create in their passion. It is more like aeonic time required for the creation of gems and precious metals; an embowelled sidereal time in which the female knows she is superior to the male and will eventually swallow him up again. The effect is that of starlight carried over into daytime . . . In this extraordinary unicellular language of the female we have a blinding, gemlike consciousness which disperses the ego like stardust. The great female corpus rises up from its sleepy marine depths in a naked push towards the sun. The sun is at zenith—permanently at zenith.

33

Henry Miller at Louveciennes, 1933

Lawrence Durrell, Paris 1937

Larry Durrell, whom I met through Henry Miller: "What first struck me were his eyes, a Mediterranean blue, keen, sparkling, seer, child, and old man . . . Under the golden tanned skin, the blond hair, the sea-bottom eyes, behind the poetic gestures, mellow and human, he has found a cataract of words, a universe of nuances, shadows, quarter-tones. . . . He is like a sailor, a mountaineer who has been visited by revelations." *

Antonin Artaud—poet, letter-writer—who had such a strong influence on the theater later. "The theater for him is a place to shout pain, anger, hatred, to enact the violence in us. The most violent life can burst from terror and death. He talked about the ancient rituals of blood. The power of contagion. How we have lost the magic of contagion. Ancient religion knew how to enact rituals which made faith and ecstasy contagious. The power of ritual was gone. He wanted to give this to the theater."

Dr. Otto Rank in his studio in Paris, 1933

Antonin Artaud as the monk
in Carl Dreyer's film
The Passion of Joan of Arc, 1929

The psychiatrist, Otto Rank. Rank was a very learned, erudite man who brought to bear upon psychoanalysis a tremendous understanding of creativity, especially in his book, *Art and Artist*. "His faith never died, nor his capacity to feel, to respond. He never hardened, never became calloused. I trusted and accepted his thought."

Conrad Moricand, the astrologer, who "believes himself to be the last of the Mohicans, a faded, high-cheeked Indian transplanted from a lost continent, whitened by long research in the Bibliothèque Nationale where he studied esoteric writings. He has a slow walk like a somnambulist enmeshed in the past and unable to walk into the present."

---

*The material enclosed in quotation marks is taken from Anaïs's diaries, unless otherwise indicated.

My first really passionate love for a writer was for D. H. Lawrence.
Reading him was a discovery for me.
His descriptions of emotions, sensations, instincts, ambivalences;
all the obscure and elusive parts of experience
were an illumination of the path I wanted to follow.
My first book was a study of Lawrence. I called it an unprofessional study,
because I was very well aware of having dropped out of school early,
and of being self-taught—no academic.

Defending and explaining D. H. Lawrence then gave me my own orientation. I was planning my course. I also took a stand as a critic. "The business of the mind is first and foremost the pure joy of knowing and comprehending, the pure joy of consciousness."

It is not a bad sign for a young writer to choose a model, for if this choice is genuine it indicates an affinity and helps the young writer find where he stands. I find young writers today too eager to disclaim any influences, not to pay homage to those who helped them set their course. I have no desire to claim that as a writer I was born in a cabbage patch.

D. H. Lawrence was an important influence because he sought a language for instinct, emotion, intuition, the most inarticulate parts of ourselves. From Lawrence I learned that naked truth is unbearable to most, and that art is our most effective way of overcoming human resistance to truth.

36

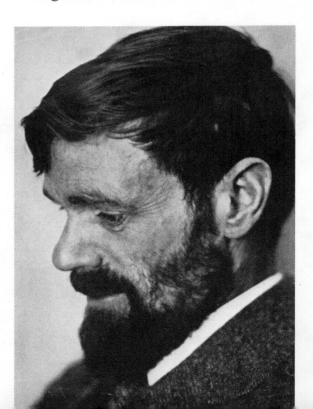

The Femininity Of D. H. Lawrence Emphasized By Woman Writer

BY WAVERLEY LEWIS ROOT

D. H. LAWRENCE: An Unprofessional Study, by Anais Nin. E. W. Titus, Paris.

That a woman should undertake to interpret D. H. Lawrence is not surprising; there was a great deal of the woman in Lawrence, as Miss Nin points out in this book. There must be something of the man in Miss Nin also, for she acquits herself with credit of the male task of analysis and comprehension from the male intellectual angle rather than from the female intuitive side.

Nevertheless there remain faults in her work (or, rather, lacunae) which are probably to be explained by the fact of her sex. She dissects Lawrence's work, and puts before us the diverse elements of his writing and of his being; but the task of synthesis has been too much for her. Perhaps, being a woman, she saw

D. H. Lawrence

no need for it. Certainly there is no indication in her book that she felt it necessary to unite all of her details into one whole which should give us the unity that is D. H. Lawrence. A man would have felt that need and would have tried, rather successfully or not, to fill it.

If the more limited talents of woman fail when she tries to attempt the work of the male, it is equally true that a man who has an admixture of feminine traits can always beat woman at her own game. Thus Lawrence. He was, as Miss Nin points out, feminine at many points. He was fundamentally intuitive as women are, and sensitive in a woman's way to the world about him—feeling, that is, before he comprehended. But he had the advantage of being, at the same time, thoroughly male. He did not stop, as the woman would, with the simple intuition. His feeling probed deeper, or, more exactly, it was multi-dimensional. A woman's intuition goes quickly to the point and seizes the uncomprehended essence of the phenomenon to which it applies itself. But a man questions what intuition tells him. He realizes the existence of plural truths, he knows that no question is so simple as to have only one answer, and at the same time that intuition may carry him to a perception of an essence, he feels other approaches to that essence, feels even the simultaneously-existing contradictions of it. In terms of mental geometry, woman's mind measure planes, man's mind solids.

That is because man doubts. Doubting Thomas was a male. Woman never doubts. That is her weakness in living, and her strength in argument. A woman would not have touched the wound of Christ. She would have believed in his resurrection and been sure of her belief, or she would have derided him and been sure in her derision.

Miss Nin does not not doubt either. She is an admirer of Lawrence (and rightly so), but for that reason her book lacks qualities that a man might have given it. It is not a criticism, but an appreciation. Miss Nin feels with Lawrence and understands him with her senses; she has not tried to do more than to present him from this angle, and her book is valuable, thus taken.

With her occasional critical estimates I do not always agree. I do not think *Lady Chatterley's Lover* was Lawrence's greatest novel, as does Miss Nin. I do not think that we may have to wait one hundred years for an appreciation of

WOMAN AUTHOR whose book on D. H. Lawrence has just been published in Paris by E. W. Titus.

Lawrence, as she suggests. Lawrence reaped full appreciation during his lifetime. His importance is accepted by the only people whose opinion matters. The fact that the United States Customs Service does not approve of Lawrence has no significance. Finally, I think that Miss Nin gives too much weight to Lawrence's own interpretation of depths of character; she seems to see in his two "psychological" works an explanation at once of the workings of the unconscious mind in general, and of Lawrence's unconscious mind in particular (although, it might be pointed out, it would be a contradiction in terms for Lawrence to be able to explain his own unconscious). These two books of Lawrence are magnificent poetry, but they are psychologically valueless, except as case material. They express in literary terms the feeling Lawrence had about the depths of the human soul, but they cannot be used as analytical measuring sticks.

Lawrence was a great poet, who chose to cast his poetry into the more difficult mold of prose. It is as a poet, that is, as a sensual artist primarily, an intellectual artist only secondarily, that he is to be comprehended. Miss Nin has understood this, even if she has not expressed herself in exactly this way, and has given us, not the definitive work on Lawrence, but nevertheless a book of considerable value.

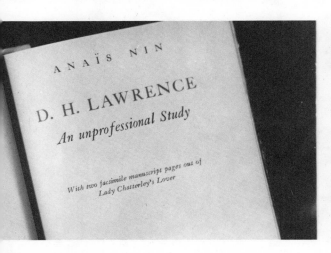

37

I often ask myself
why I began to edit the published diary
in 1931.

I was living in a lovely place where I was a lonely writer . . .
I knew no one else who was writing.

And so 1931—the year Henry Miller and his wife, June,
came to visit me in Louveciennes—was really
the beginning of the interesting part of my life.

As soon as Miller appeared at the door one felt elated by his presence.

Henry Miller: The thing that distinguished you in a group is that you were the listener—but your listening was always eloquent.... In the last few years, one sees quite a few writings either about you or quotations from you about dreams and the dream life, but I feel they haven't really understood what you mean.

I don't think you want people to be living, walking around, in a dream state while conscious, do you?

Anaïs Nin: I meant that we could arrive at a state where what we dreamed at night would be like the blueprint for what we wished to fulfill. And if we understand the dream as an acceptance of the secret self, then we know what the secret self is, and then we can fulfill this secret self.

I just finished this book about writing and writers, and I said if only people trusted the artist to do the dreaming, then, instead of taking drugs, they might look at a painting for a long time, or watch a mobile for a long time, and if they looked very deeply, they would be set off on their own dreaming.

Henry Miller: Instead of what they do now, trying to understand the artist and his work with the intellect....

Anaïs Nin: Yes.... and I always give the example of dreaming about the houseboat, then getting it, then writing the stories, then living in it, and then going on....

Gonzalo More's drawing of Anaïs's houseboat *La Belle Aurore*

First it was a fantasy. But you're right when you say people don't understand what I mean. They say my writing is dreamlike, that is, not of life. And I'm always trying to say the dream is related to life, it nourishes it, it frees us.

"To capture the dream of the unconscious, one has to start with the key, and the key is the dream. The novelist's task is to pursue this dream, to unravel its meaning: the goal is to reach the relation of dream to life; the suspense is

in finding this which leads to a deeper significance of our acts. I discovered that the dream has to be expanded, recreated, could not be told literally, for then it became as flat and one-dimensional as representational realism. One has to find a language for it, a way of describing atmosphere, the colors and textures in which it moved. The writer's role is to express what we cannot express. He is our virtuoso; he can help us out of our prison of inarticulateness. The writer's role is not ornamental; it is to teach us to speak as we feel and as we see.''

One night in a café
Larry and Henry and I sat a whole night discussing writing.
It was the first time it occurred to me
that I had to take a path of my own,
go my own way . . .
because I really didn't agree with Larry's idea
that you have to write a *Hamlet* first, before you write well,
and I didn't quite agree with Henry either
who was denying the personal motivation in his work—
I wanted to write in a personal way, very close to experience,
and what I felt to be the difference
between what a woman has to say
and what a man has to say.
Perhaps Henry and Larry will go the same way,
but I will have to go another, the woman's way.

44

Wind-up of letter to father !!
"Papa chéri, c'est ta fille
qui te parle et qui te demande."
Anaïs

"Si je pouvais faire servir
mes pattes de mouche."

Heureusement mon journal
n'est pas un album !

25 ¢ a week — 12 dollars a year —
from uncles + aunts. "mon
Dieu! si cela pouvais con-
tinuer ?" (Pathétique)

Pour moi chaque jour
c'est une nouveauté et il me
semble que mon caractere
change toujours.

Son nom est André dans
mon reve car je ne connais
personne de ce nom.
(George Sand + Pierre Loti — et 14!)

"ma Soeur" by Joaquinito. — !!
"Coeur d'Or". — "je pense mêler
beaucoup de mystère etc."
"Pages choisies des grands
écrivains" — Turgenev (Puffin)
J'ai perdu l'illusion de
l'amour que m'a donné
Geo. Sand (thru Turgenev!)
Un de ces jours je devrais
dire : "Mon journal, je
suis arrivée au fond".

Watching rose petals fall —
"alors, je me demande qui est-ce
qui ramasse les petales qui se
detache de mon coeur".
mon Dieu! suis-je déja si vieille q
je ne puis servir à rien ?"
Suis-je comme tout le monde ?
Voilà la question!
Alex. Dumas & Geo. Sand sont les
premiers qui ont ouvert pour moi la
porte du jardin inconnu de "L'amour"
Maman: "Fille de ton père, mauvaise
graine va !" (???)
Je sais bien que maman ne com
prends pas ce qui passe en moi.
Que je vous aime, mon journal car
chaque fois que je vous parle je souff
moins et je me comprends mieux.
"Je serai pourrai etre heureuse ave
une plume et un morceau de pain
de pain quotidien. (Letter to father)
(marvellous letter!) Rousseau et la
plume! Moi je sais que poussiere,
faites pour etre marché dessus.
(type out whole letter)
Je suis sur cette terre &, personne n'a besoin de moi.
Je suis ce qu'on appelle "quelqu'un de trop"- et je le sens....
Pour quoi vis-je ?
Si l'on appelle romantique quelqu'un q

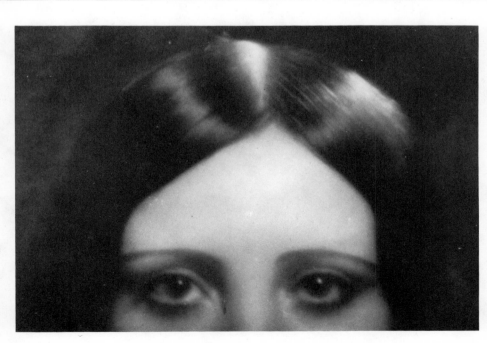

Saturday

Anaïs:

Just received your two letters and realize that you did get the second letter sent to Switzerland. If the typewriter has a standard american keyboard I certainly will be able to use it, and even if it is somewhat different I can no doubt get adjusted. My desire for the regular keyboard is because I type very fast, and if I have to think where the keys are I get lost. The first letter says you are sending it and the later one asks — can you use it? I dispatched a long letter last night.

That you found the old novel good in parts and that you think it could be doctored and made publishable is swell. Sure, I would be delighted if you would go over it and prune it. Even if only a hundred pages remain, and they are good, why O.K. Perhaps I could reciprocate some time by doing the same for you. Go ahead and make a stab at it. Nothing but good can result. I can always trim down to french proportions. I think too, I would agree with you on whatever you wanted to cut. And after you get thru with it, I believe I would have sufficient enthusiasm to make further revisions my-self. I remember the dream passage — I know I could improve there too. You get me excited about it.

Man's objectivity may be an imitation of this God,
so detached from us and human emotions. . . .
Woman was born mother, mistress, wife, sister.
She was born to give birth to life, and not to insanity.
Is it man's separateness, his so-called objectivity, that has made him
lose contact . . . and then his reason?
Woman was born to be the connecting link between man and his human self—
she gives union, communion, communication, . . . art.

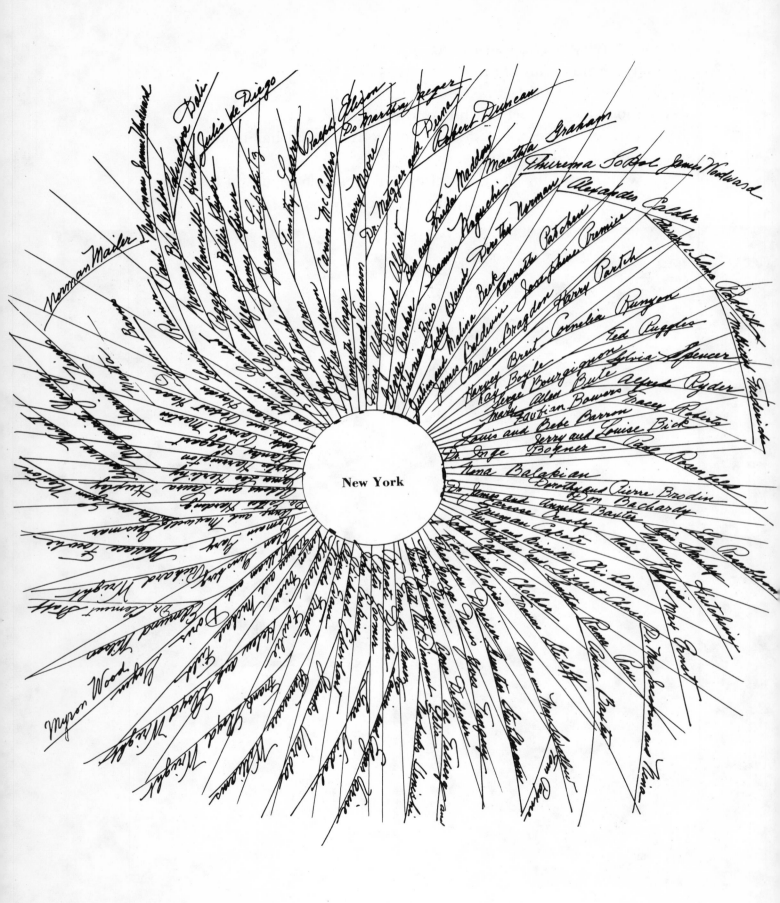

*New York was a tremendous,
violent contrast to Paris.*

Completely uprooted, I found it at first an impersonal city.
And then, I began to know another New York: the fraternity of artists;
the world I always depended on, was created once again.

Frances Steloff's bookshop, The Gotham Book Mart, was important to all of us. It was a favorite meeting place for writers and artists, and it was there I met the sculptor Noguchi and Edmund Wilson.

"Frances has antennae, and a gift for friendship. She welcomed the unusual, the uncommercial, the avant-garde. As a result, everything converged to her store—small magazines, rare books, special unique people looking for special books. . . .

It is almost like being in a private library, with a familiar natural disorder."

Anaïs Nin: You were very friendly to unknown writers, and then, the war was coming and we felt we didn't want to leave our books in Europe. So we wrote you, asking if we could send you our books. You said yes, immediately, and we thought that was wonderful.

Frances Steloff: Of course, it was always my feeling that the next best thing to being a writer was to help those that were.

Anaïs Nin: Then we had a wonderful time, if you remember, when the publishers wouldn't take my two books, and I decided to get a printing press and do them myself. And you lent me money for the press.

Frances Steloff: I remember that part so vividly. I lent you a hundred dollars, and then I bought a hundred dollars worth of books in advance. I knew that I could sell them. I had great faith, in those days. And even though I hadn't read anything of yours, I knew it would sell. In that way you were able to buy the press . . . and you worked so hard.

I loved working with my hands; feeling the weight of the tray.
I really loved looking at it,
hearing the purring of the machine,
and seeing the pages comes out.

Winter of Artifice took eight months to hand-set. I forget how long it took to print. *Under a Glass Bell* was also set by hand. We were printing Ian Hugo's engravings in the William Blake method—which means that every time you

print an engraving you have to wipe off the ink, and ink it again. So, it was a very slow, romantic, medieval process that we really loved.

"While I have enjoyed the informality of the diary writing, I also enjoyed compressing and cutting the short stories in *Under a Glass Bell* until they were gemlike. I would not change one word today, twenty years later." The third book we did was a color engraving on wooden plates, *House of Incest*. It was not hand-set, but it had original engravings which we printed. . . . The whole process was very beautiful, very strangely satisfying, for a writer is always dealing, in a way, with abstractions.

I'm probably the only writer who wept when I got a formal, commercial contract with a publisher, because I felt the books wouldn't be as beautiful. Instead of celebrating, I wept.

"My first vision of earth was water veiled.
I am of the race of men and women
who see all things through this curtain of sea,
and my eyes are the color of water."

Anaïs Nin: After that time I had to struggle with the writing. Now, the minute Edmund Wilson reviewed *Under the Glass Bell*, all the publishers called me. The next day, in fact. And that was the beginning of a little attempt at acceptance.

Frances Steloff: I knew it would mean a great deal because he was a most respected critic in literature.

Anaïs Nin: He was a very generous man. He was very generous about the portrait I made of him in the *Diary*, which was a little severe.

53

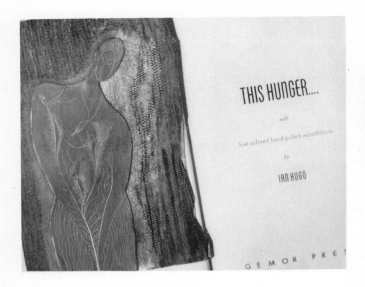

THIS HUNGER....

with

five colored hand-pulled woodblocks

by

IAN HUGO

GEMOR PRESS

SOLAR BARQUE
By
ANAIS NIN

Illustrations By
PETER LOOMER

winter
of
artifice

anaïs
nin

ANAIS NIN

THIS HUNGER....

54

ANAIS NIN

HOUSE OF INCEST

"His was a world of power and certitudes, solidities and aggressiveness. Strength and willfulness."

The pieces in this collection belong to a peculiar genre sometimes cultivated by the late Virginia Woolf. They are half short stories, half dreams, and they mix a sometimes exquisite poetry with a homely realistic observation. They take place in a special world, a world of feminine perception and fancy, which is all the more curious and charming for being innocently international. . . .

The imagery does convey something and is always appropriate. The spun glass is also alive: it is the abode of a secret creature. Half woman, half childlike spirit, she shops, employs servants, wears dresses, suffers the pains of childbirth, yet is likely at any moment to be volatilized into a superterrestrial being who feels things that we cannot feel.

But perhaps the main thing to say is that Miss Nin is a very good artist, as perhaps none of the literary Surrealists are.

Edmund Wilson's review of *Under the Glass Bell* in the *New Yorker*

Anaïs Nin: Older authors, I think, are more generous than the young ones.

Frances Steloff: I think so . . . I think so—

Anaïs Nin: They take their lives philosophically and accept themselves as they are.

Frances Steloff: Yes, and they don't expect too much.

Edmund Wilson

Silvia Salmi

ANAIS NIN

UNDER
A
GLASS BELL

LINE ENGRAVINGS ON COPPER

by

IAN HUGO

NOGUCHI
1930

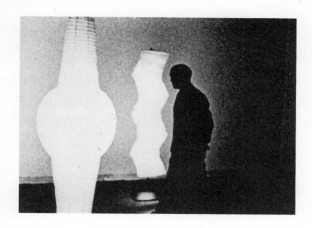

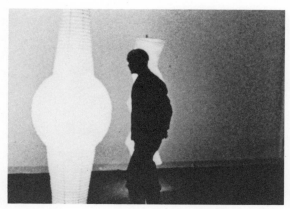

It was Noguchi's
who taught me to look at
every form with interest —

the form of a rock, or the form of a candle . . . or a dog.
It was really Noguchi who opened my eyes to form.

Noguchi:

I have this rather puritannical aversion to sculpture as merely objects for the rich.
I would very much like that sculpture be enjoyed freely by everybody.
I, from time to time, wanted to make something that everybody could own,
and this is how I got involved in making Acari lamps—
that is, papier-maché used with electricity—
and became very fascinated by the problem,
both as a luminous sculpture
and as something that would go into the homes of everybody.

59

Noguchi also did the sets for the dance theater of Martha Graham, one of the artists I most admired for her magic power to create and transform—every gesture illuminated with meaning, . . . nothing lost. . . . for the suggestiveness, the placing of the characters, the symbolic enacting. Her dance inspired a whole section of *Ladders to Fire* which I called The Party.

Martha Graham:
Dance is communication . . . and the great desire is to speak
clearly and beautifully and with inevitability.
It is the creative process.
It is out of the handling of the material of the self
that you are able to hold the stage
in the full maturity and power which that magical place demands.
The dancer is a realist. His craft teaches him to be.
Either the foot is pointed, or it is not . . .
no amount of dreaming will point it for you.
This requires discipline.
Not drill, not something imposed from without,
but discipline imposed by you yourself upon yourself.
In the studio you learn to conform, to submit yourself to the demands of your craft
so that you may finally be free.
Your goal is freedom,
but freedom may only be achieved through discipline.

60

Peter Glushanok

Maya Deren, in a frame from her film *Meshes of the Afternoon*

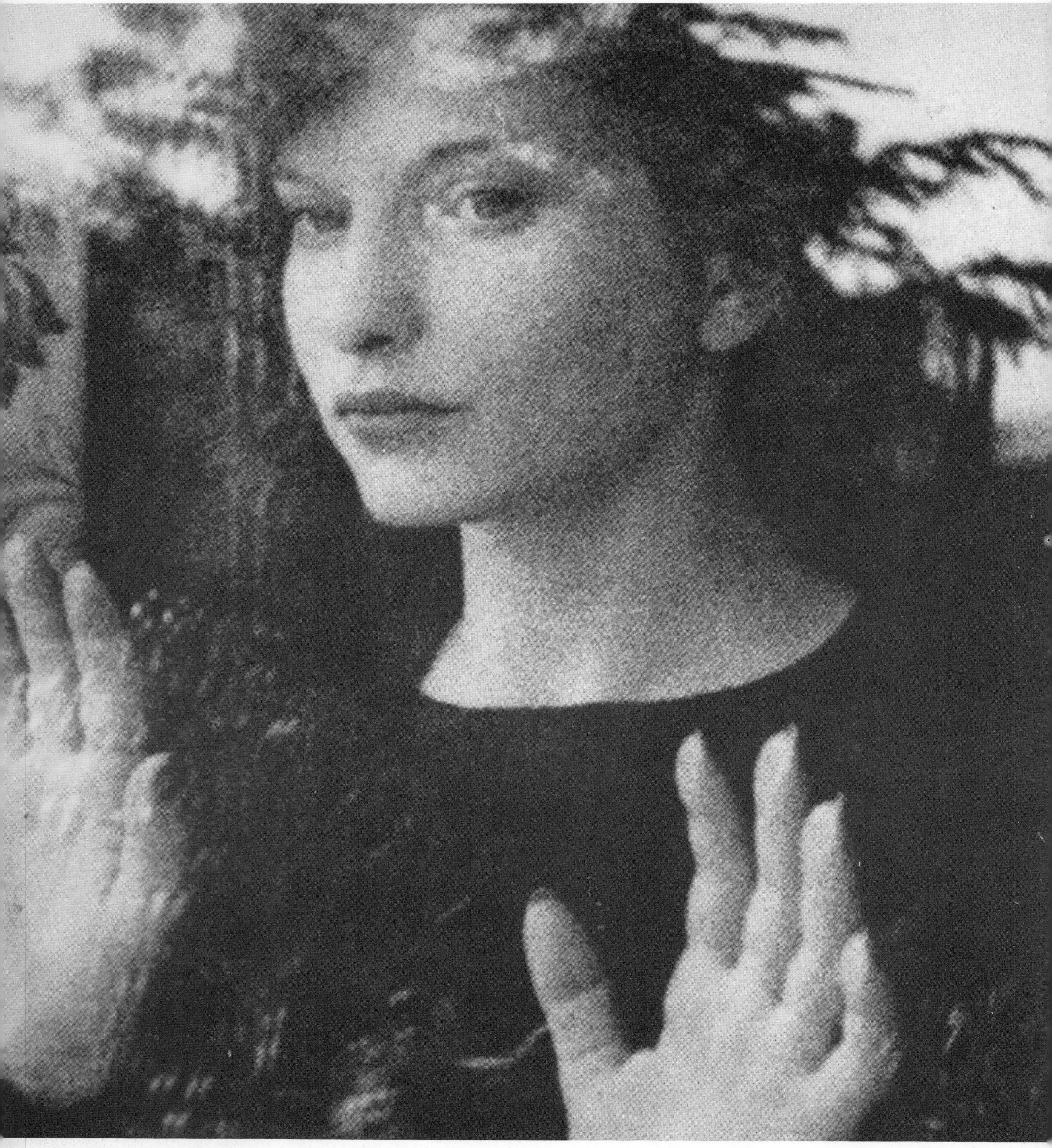

Maya Deren was a fascinating woman. She was a great influence in films and *Ritual in Transfigured Time* was probably a revolution of the art. She filmed all my friends who were individually interesting, just letting things happen. Sometimes they didn't, and sometimes what happened was quite different from what she expected.

"We believed in her as a film-maker, we had faith in her, but we began to feel she was not human.

The power of her personality, the unblinking blue eyes, the sturdy curled hair growing gypsylike in an aureole around her face; her face square and strong, like a Botticelli—round eyes, full mouth—but far stronger; her determined voice, the assertiveness and sensuality of her peasant body, her dancing, drumming: all haunted us. We spent a great deal of time talking about her. . . . We had a mixture of admiration for her energy and obstinacy and rebellion against her dominant presence."

Anaïs in Maya Deren's film *Ritual in Transfigured Time*

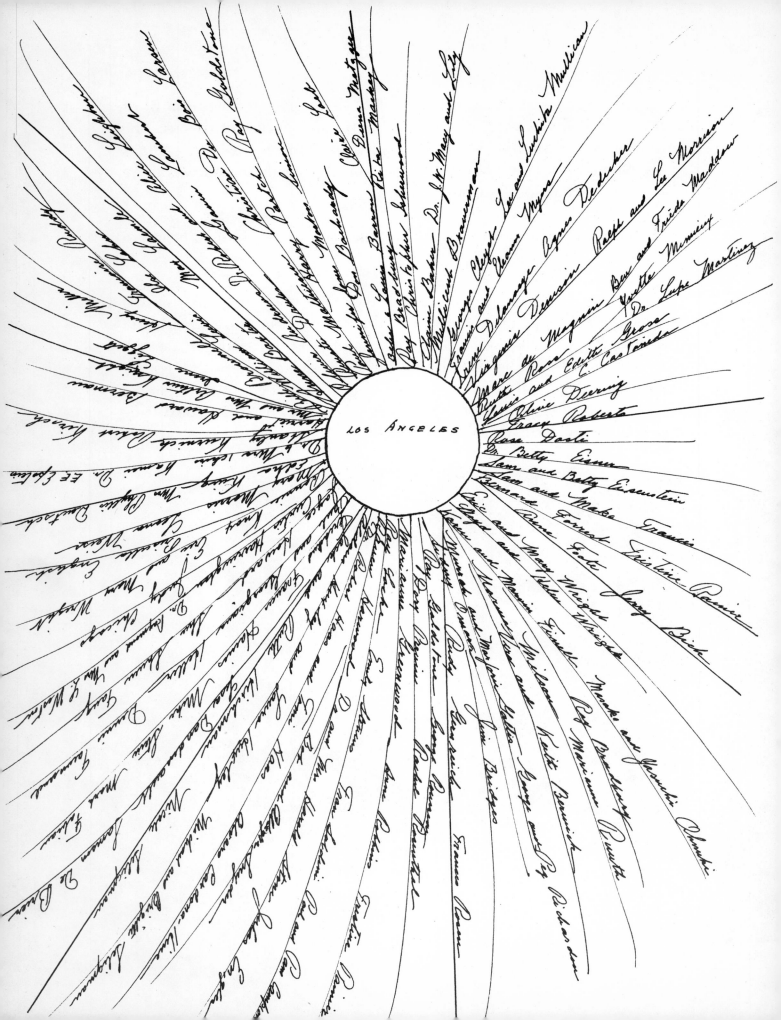

I first came out to Los Angeles looking for a city closer to nature.

Lloyd Wright, Harry Partch, Jean Varda, Renate Druks . . .

From Thailand I brought back a spirit house, which is an exact duplicate of their little houses on stilts, for their ancestral spirits. They plant this little house in their gardens and bring food for the spirits every day.

John Engstead

The spirit house reminds me of Lloyd Wright, the poet of architecture, whose imaginative work caught my interest when I first came out here. I love the houses he built, and particularly the Wayfarer's Chapel for the Swedenborgian religion, all of glass, through which you can see both the ocean and the trees. I felt that if he had been given free rein, Los Angeles might have been a city like Venice, Italy, that all the world would come to see.

66

There are some painters who give me the feeling
that I would like to live inside their paintings.
I've always had that feeling about Varda's collages. . . .
I wanted to be inside his collages
and he wanted his collages to be part of my life.
The first time I heard of Varda was in a letter Henry wrote me in New York.
A few days later I got this huge package marked,
FAN LETTER, and I opened it and saw
this marvelous collage that Henry had seen in Varda's barn and admired,
Women Reconstructing the World.
It was one of the strangest and most prophetic coincidences
because I was working on a novel about free women called *Ladders to Fire*.

There were four women in it,
and in the collage there were four women
who were almost literal descriptions of those characters.
And this is the collage:

This is the musician, carrying music on her head;
this is the abstract woman who has a great interior life, much happening inside her.
This is a woman who is like a sieve
and experience goes through the diamond-shaped opening in her dress
and comes out the other way.
And this, of course, is Stella, who is graceful and half dancer, half actress.
And so they're all there—there's Hedjda—there they are, those houses . . .

I call them "women of transportable roots," because they are very mobile, and fluid, and international.

They belong to the whole world.

Varda's letter:
"I take the liberty to send you a collage with a vain title, and if you should enjoy it, I would feel less indebted and wildly proud to return a small part of the joy I have received from the rivers of delectations which flow from your pen."

I fixed my eyes on the Varda collage.

It was as if I had stepped out of my life into a region of sand composed of crystals, of transparent women dancing in airy dresses, figures which no obstacle could stop, who could pass through walls, beings designed like sieves to allow the breeze through. Through these floating figures with openings like windows, life could flow. . . .

I escaped from the confinement of four brown walls, . . . for I acquired in these moments of contemplation of Varda's collage the certainty that such a state of life was attainable, everything that man creates being attainable, for he has invented nothing, he has transcribed his moods and visions and vistas, experiences and images.

"Where had he learned the secret of phosphorescence, of illumination, of transfiguration? Where had he learned to take the shabbiest materials and heighten them with paint, alter their shapes with scissors?"

Varda had this obsession with cloth, with little pieces of textiles that he used on his collages. One day I arrived and he walked up to me and he looked at the lining of my coat in an obsessional way, and he said: "Oh, I would love to have a little piece of that."

I really didn't say yes then, because for a women to tear the lining of a coat takes a little . . . hesitation. But the next day I did. I slashed right through it and sent Varda a piece, and it is now a part of the collage owned by Gavin Lambert; so he has a piece of my coat as well!

70

I've always felt close to Harry Partch's music, with the extraordinary instruments which he designed himself. I think he reaches the range that Eastern music does, but in his own American idiom.

"The affinity of his music with water, with the poetry of space, with fusion appealed to me.... The affinity with Oriental music which has a flowing, enveloping, oceanic rhythm. Rhythm was an essential part of Partch's music, a native contemporary rhythm."

Renate Druks made a photo collage of the masquerade party to which we were all supposed to come as our madness. My madness was to put my head in a birdcage, and out of the cage hung a long tickertape of the unconscious, ribbons of paper on which I had done a great deal of writing. This crystallized Kenneth Anger's idea for a film happening called *Inauguration of the Pleasure Dome*.

Anaïs is completing volume five of the diaries (by now this volume is already in the bookstores, and volume six, too, is now ready). I remember a letter Henry wrote to William A. Bradley, a literary agent, who suggested that she edit her diaries to make them publishable. Henry wrote:

> *Dear Mr. Bradley:*
>
> *Since you are the one who has inspired the premeditated abortion of Anaïs Nin's Journal, some pages of which have just come to my attention, I am addressing myself to you directly.*
>
> *For me it is a foregone conclusion that the Journal is a work of the highest standing, that it is indeed altogether unique. Granting that my knowledge of the world's literature is not as extensive as your own, I nevertheless challenge you to cite me a worthy parallel to it. Myself I know of none. None by any man, and most certainly none by a woman. If it were due only to its uniqueness as a female contribution my unflinching endorsement of it would be entirely justified. But it does not owe its value or importance to this aspect in the least. It is a unique human contribution, doubly so because the female has been most naturally more reticent, more reluctant to expose her soul. . . . It is a tremendous cross-section of our life today. A tremendous revelation of the evolution of a soul. . . . You ask her to sit down and make a warm stew of her past in order to tickle the prurient public. . . . What motivates your conduct is the public. The public, however, can damn well take care of itself. As can the publisher. It is the author who requires the most of you, rightfully and justly. . . . Any dolt can feed the public what it wants. Any pimp can pander to the perverted interests of the publishers. Everything begins and everything ends with the author—the public and the printer are simply accessories before God.*
>
> *Let me tell you what I, an author, an impractical person, think ought to be done [with the journal]. I say after mature deliberation—print the whole god-damned thing!*

She takes care of her quite massive correspondence. Of course, we try to film as many events as possible, but for one reason or another there are many that we missed. She and Rupert generally go to the Santa Monica beach of a fine Sunday—walk, bask in the sun, rendezvous with beach-loving friends. I was eager to get that, but somehow. . . .

I did get up to San Francisco to attend one of her lectures at the University of California at Berkeley. Not to film—the expense would have been staggering at this point—but to participate by screening a small section of the film in progress. Under John Pearson's expert direction, the lecture became a weekend "furrawn." Some 1,500 people jammed Zellerbach Hall—young and old, male and female, many coming from out of state and paying 35 dollars for a weekend of lecture, diary readings, poetry readings, but mostly to see her in the flesh. And in the crush to the stage that followed her talks, to see her more closely, hear her, perhaps touch her, I seemed to sense an almost religious rapture.

What follows is a day in the life of Anaïs Nin: her work, correspondence, tea with an interviewer (me), being visited by a writer or a group of students, an evening out—to a movie, an art show, a concert—an evening in—a chamber-music musicale every few weeks—being quiet, taking a swim in the little pool.

*Perhaps I felt the right time
had come, that I was
ripe as a writer, a craftsman;*
and I could really face the difficulties of editing a diary during my own
lifetime and during the lifetimes of most of the people concerned in it. When
I really began the work of editing, the difficulty was to sustain a continuity of
the inner journey and not worry so much about a few facts that had to be left
out. As long as there was an emotional continuity, a development you could
really follow, I felt that was satisfactory.

What I publish is about half of what I've written. Still, there's very little of the essential left out because I think there is enough left to read between the lines and to complete the story.

Now, suppose I had put in every word; you would have missed the real purpose of the diary, which is the inner journey of free association.

What you feel most intensely at the moment, you write about most strongly, and the whole thing acquires a living quality.

I open the original journal, and then I type. And then I might think a certain portion can't be included because it may hurt the person I'm portraying. I try to portray them so deeply that I go beyond judgment, seeking the motivation for what they do—which just means acceptance.

This must have been a strong element in the diaries because I never received any protests really, except perhaps one or two characters. And these were not protests of how true my portrait was, but simply that there were details they didn't want revealed.

If I am blocked due to something I'm concealing, I try first to find out what it is I am afraid to say—a revelation or a secret fear of being destructive or harming others. But there are other times when I'm stuck in a very strange way: I don't quite know my own direction.

In that case I either put on some music like Debussy, which restores the flow—you know that impressionistic oceanic flow—or else I read Proust, which has the same effect on me. A few words of Proust will set me aflow again; it makes me catch my rhythm again. If I'm tired, if the block comes from fatigue, then swimming and playing with my dog and working in the garden help me.

But there are times when I'm like a musician who has suddenly lost his rhythm and has to stop and catch it again. The singing of the mockingbirds became a very important melody accompanying my work and my life here. It's such a beautiful, varied song, and I became so interested that in between my writing sessions I go out and record them. That has had a

wonderful lyrical effect, because I've never liked my pedestrian, down-to-earth writing. I always wanted my writing to levitate.

I was always as interested in the work of all the artists around me as I was in my own. If there were no other writers, it would be pathetic! We were interdependent and nourished each other; the musicians helped me, and the writers. I wanted a world full of good writers.

82

This is today's correspondence. I spend a long time answering these letters because the first letter I ever wrote was to Djuna Barnes and she never answered. So I made a vow that I would never leave a letter unanswered. Sometimes, instead of a letter, I get a letter collage—like this one by Virginia Ballentine, using all my favorite words: transmute, transform, transpose, imponderable, wordless, essence, beyond, mobile, expand, cities, diffuse, mystery, miracles, sorcery—you can read them by the hour.

Then she has a little piece of music,
"Trans-Siberian Voyage,"
a voyage I always wanted to take.
The whole thing is underground.
You see, plants and grass are growing up here on top;
then all this happens below, in the unconscious:
"process, flowing, creation,
luminous, alchemy, mirrors, dissolve . . ."

*The publication of the Diaries
opened up to me a realm of people
I did not even know existed,*
revealed to me by their letters, even sending me their diaries. When they
write me, they really want to be present—as friends who will come and talk
about their lives. They immediately feel on a footing of friendship and
sharing. They feel they owe me that too, for me to know them in a deep way.

Lou Andreas-Salomé

I can tell you so many reasons why I love Lou Andreas-Salomé: not only because she created the kind of freedom that women today demand, but because she created it for herself in an impossible period, at a time when women were not even allowed to study in universities. And she was also the first woman psychoanalyst. At the age of fifty she decided that the answers to the problems she had thought were philosophical, were psychological. So then, with the encouragement of Freud, she became an analyst. The other thing I love about her is that she was really a muse. Everyone knew this.

Everyone that knew her was so inspired to reach their highest selves with her, that this was part of the seduction. I mean, aside from being a beautiful woman there was always something awakened, and stirred . . .

Rilke admitted very often that she had set him free . . . expanded his vision. She was the one who announced the end of a relationship, which was very unusual for that time. She said to Rilke, Now the passion is spent, the relationship is over. And she ended it.

88

To me she is a heroine who didn't wait for the right time and didn't wait for other women to think as she did. She just went ahead and created her own freedom. She had no guilt. She also had a tremendously rebellious spirit which led her almost automatically to break all taboos: she rebelled against the way that marriage was set up, the way the lover relationship was set up, the way philosophy was set up in that time. She rebelled against religion when she was very young. That's why I consider her a contemporary heroine.

Of course there are other women that I love. I don't know if you know Leslie Blanch's *Wilder Shores of Love*, about four Englishwomen who decided to turn their backs on their cultures and integrate themselves into the life of the Middle East. One was, of course, Mrs. Richard Burton. Another was Lady Jane Digby, who married an Arab and led a perfectly Arab wife's life. She was a great horsewoman and even learned to raid tourist parties. She lived exactly according to her husband's beliefs—washed his feet when he came back from the desert—and was a beautiful woman until the age of seventy when she died.

Another was Isabelle Eberhardt, a remarkable Russian girl who ran away from her immigrant life in southern France and went to live as a boy with the Arabs. She dressed as a boy, lived in caravans, was a friend of Lyautey, and was considered a link between Arabs and the French, and they trusted her to exchange messages and understanding. The Arabs respected her anonymity so much that although they knew she was a woman they never let on.

Astrologers announced her death, and it is one case they proved themselves right. They said she would die—drowned in the desert. And she did die, at the age of twenty-four, in a flash flood in the desert—and left a diary which still has not been translated into English.

Oh! and there's a fourth! Aimée Dubucq de Rivery, a cousin of the Empress Josephine. She was stolen by the Turks and placed in a harem, and from the harem she caused a revolution in Turkey—which shows you what women can do anywhere, at any time, in any place.

Caresse Crosby, the "mouvement perpetuelle," due to her saying yes to all of life. Caresse, still saying yes.

Caresse Crosby: Yes, and never no, was our answer to the fabulous 20s and 30s.

Anaïs Nin: I loved Caresse's Women Against War, her Citizens of the World idea. She created her world passport and flew her one-world flag from her castle, Roccasinibalda, in Italy.

Caresse Crosby: My idea is to create an atmosphere here where the poet and the philosopher and the artist can give ideas that will lead the world to peace and sanity. I believe really that the national unit is outmoded, and that the politician can lead us nowhere. We need men of ideas, men of vision, and men of compassion.

The great concern of my diaries is with the psychic life:
the life of the soul, of the spirit, the concern with human values,
how to break down that alienation
which we create by terrible taboos on revelation and on human life experiences.
We never used to talk—
there was a period when people didn't even talk together.

I'm in the midst of writing volume five
which brings in themes from all the other volumes.
It includes my experience of taking LSD.
I was invited to do it by Dr. Oscar Janiger as an experiment.
Dr. Janiger wanted to use a musician, a scientist, a writer.
He said the writer would be better able to tell what it was like.
I was very curious to see whether there was a world that I had never penetrated,
that only LSD could give me.
I'm always curious about an unknown world.

The memory of the LSD experience is very clear and I wrote the whole thing out—
a long, long, long, long reverie.
And then I compared it to see
whether the images brought on by LSD were similar
to images and sensations and impressions I had already described.
And I found them in my work—particularly in the first book I wrote,
a prose poem, *The House of Incest*, which was made up of dreams.
The material was so like what was brought on by LSD
that it proved my point that this dream world is a world accessible to the poet,
accessible to the artist.
If we wouldn't belittle the artist and the poet so much,
we wouldn't need drugs to reach these visions.

One of the most marvelous things,
which is almost indescribable
and probably only happened to mystics,
was when I found myself turning into gold.
Suddenly, I turned myself into gold—
and it is a sensation I've never been able to describe
except, perhaps, as it might be compared to making love.

92

Now my whole effort, in my work and in my life, was to return, to reconstruct those bridges that had been violently cut. And, of course, as the diaries developed, I began to see that everything was opening up into the world.

Suddenly, the world answers the writer and she's not alone anymore, the work is not a solitary chant anymore, it becomes universal. It happened as soon as I was able to share the diary, and I was really very much afraid to do that, fearing, as we all fear, not to be loved, but judged.

When I overcame that fear, and finally published them, I found myself in complete communion with a whole world of people who revealed themselves to me in their letters, who send me their diaries. . . .

So the last few years have been extraordinary, and I think it fulfills the dream of every artist—really to contact the world, and to rebuild those bridges so that other people will also realize that they don't have to be isolated, and they don't have to be locked in the solitary chamber of the neurotic.

So I began on a desert island,
and then found my way back into universal communion,
particularly with the new consciousness of the young.

94

Jill Krementz

It was during this time that I received a telephone call inviting me to join in a challenging adventure in education, the International College in Los Angeles, which was to be an international guild of masters and students—learners. I signed on with great enthusiasm as dean of the masters program and to set up a Center for Learning Resources. Then I called on my heroes and heroines, mostly dropouts unaffiliated with the educational establishment, to take on some qualified apprentices, students. Anaïs, along with Bucky Fuller, Larry Durrell, John Whitney, George Leonard, hopped aboard. Within a short space of time, Anaïs had accepted ten students who visited her periodically at her home to work at diary writing. One afternoon, she reminisced:

97

My own education misfired,
and it lead me to become interested in the problems of the individual.
I was eleven years old when I was brought to New York
and knew only Spanish and French.
I was put in public school, and what happened is
that I immediately developed a passion for the English language—
a passionate curiosity, a passionate interest
which usually only a foreigner will experience.
Because I didn't take English for granted,
I felt like an explorer,
discovering it had an infinite variety of words.
Learning the new language was like an adventure;
every word was opening up a new dimension,
a new country, a new feeling,
and so I was discovering
the character of my new country from its language.

I brought these words to class, these new words, and I was always asking, Why can't we use this and why do we say that? But my teacher said at the time, "I am very sorry that you are taking that route, because it's a very pretentious and literary English that you're getting interested in." She said too, "All these words are quite useless, and I would rather you go around the corner and buy a bunch of magazines and learn colloquial English so that you can communicate with your fellow-classmates and with people, because you're getting into a precious and pretentious use of English."

So I got no encouragement for my passionate feeling for the English language. As I matured I began to realize the problem of the teacher too. She must have felt that she couldn't take time away from the other fifty or sixty students in the class to pay attention to just one student.

But I think that if she had spent just that extra minute encouraging that small area which fascinated me so, I might not have become the original dropout. I left grammar school and never went on to high school. Instead I proceeded to educate myself. I was lucky to have been born into a house full of books, so that reading was a very natural thing. I went to the public library and read alphabetically from A to Z—just everything that came on the shelf. That was my education.

Then, at sixteen and seventeen I got a little bit lonely with my self-discipline and my constant passion for language. So I went to Columbia University and decided to take an extension course in the short story. They started to tell me that the stories I was writing had no beginning and no middle and no end—something they're still telling me today. I suddenly realized I couldn't write a story the way the pattern was set, and so again I dropped out. But after all this, I ended up giving a lecture on style at Harvard a few years ago!

As a foreigner, not taking a language for granted, I went much deeper into it, explored it, and asked for all its possibilities. It was a passion. If we could develop in each child just that little area of passion, it would naturally spread into other areas of learning. With me, interest in language inevitably led me into other areas: I knew there was a language of the painter, a language of the workman, a language of the fisherman, and a language of the lovers. So you see, language takes you everywhere.

Although I have always loved the concept of sharing whatever I know or have learned—which is, I suppose, a teacher—I never became one because I left school at the sixth grade. What appealed to me about the International College was the chance to concentrate on one person, and to spend time enough to see the efflorescence, to find out in what area they have this passion which is very important for growth.

99

I remember my first student asking me, "Will you give me an assignment while you're away on a lecture tour?" I answered that I wouldn't think of it, that I wanted first to find out what the student really wanted to write, that I wasn't going to tell her what to write. In my case, the teacher tried to keep everyone at the same level; she tried to force me into a colloquialism which never interested me, because I felt it didn't communicate. So now, as a teacher, I have a chance to search for the basic potential, to try to awaken the unique potential in each person.

A group of young writers from UCLA came over to visit.

Girl: In a quotation you say that anger poisons one. I wondered whether you thought it could ever be a creative emotion.

Anaïs: There are different kinds of anger. There is a kind of anger that is toxic and ineffectual; and there's a creative anger, rebellion: the rebellion against puritanism, against certain suffocating situations for a woman. Writers are rebels.

In volume five I have a great deal of anger about the silence that surrounded my work in the fifties. That didn't do me any good, because there was nothing I could do to change it. I can see now that the time just wasn't right. So my anger would have done nothing but make me bitter. Bitter people, angry people, are corroded by their anger.

Girl: What happened to the parts that you cut out of your diary?

Anaïs: Oh, they're all there. I open the original diary and I type and then I say, This part can't go in because it's about my mother, or something like that. And then I go on. I just leave it out.

Girl: It's amazing how well it holds together.

Anaïs: Yes, because I tried to be true to the emotional development, to the feelings about life and reactions to events so that there is a continuity in that, even if the facts and the chronology are not complete.

At about the same time Anaïs took part in a seminar on D. H. Lawrence given by Lawrence Durrell at Cal Tech:

Lawrence Durrell: It is difficult to describe how dismal our lives were in the kind of society depicted by D. H. Lawrence, with those two great terrifying fears: one of syphilis and the other of pregnancy—which absolutely ruined all lovemaking. And I think part of Lawrence's struggle would have been resolved automatically had he been here now talking to you. Do you see, he would say, "Well, it's not quite the same case anymore," and he would probably modify some of his whip blasts.

But you had to face that problem too. You say you nearly lost your family because of writing a book about Lawrence. And *Tropic of Cancer*—when I smuggled copies into England to distribute to other writers, I was facing two years in prison, firm. And they wouldn't print my *Black Book* and leave the four-letter words in, even though there were only three! But tell us about the reaction of your family.

Anaïs: Oh, it was simply a condemnation for my having written about Lawrence. They were ashamed. . . .

Durrell: But you come from a family of artists!

Anaïs: But this was in the period when people threatened to burn Lawrence's paintings, when the police visited all his friends in England to whom he had sent copies of *Lady Chatterley*. In other words, the persecution was very real; it was not an imaginary persecution. And then the reviewers said terrible things about his work, even the Bloomsbury group. Nobody stood by him at all.

Yet Lawrence was a Puritan. He would quarrel with friends who separated and married someone else. Wasn't it Aldington who was living with one woman and then married another? And Lawrence was incensed by that. He was a Puritan. To call himself the "priest of love" was. . . .

Durrell: It was very dangerous.

Anaïs: I think there's a difference between Lawrence and Miller in that sense. Miller was trying to crack the Puritan ethic. He wasn't trying to be a "priest of love." He was writing a comedy of love.

When I was twenty I found myself in Lawrence. He does create a reality in which you can live. In reading *Lady Chatterley's Lover*, I felt awakened to the senses, but I thought this was a question of generation and that the book wouldn't have as great an impact today. So I was amazed to hear recently from a young woman student of mine who is just twenty years old, that she felt the same reaction.

Musicale at Home

It could have gone on and on; I'd just as lief it had—and damn the expense! But Anaïs was much more responsible and reminded me that we should close, we had so much already. We could always pick up new material in the future and—together with the unused material of our current film—make another one. So that's how diaries work! How, I wonder sotto voce, *will I appear in the diaries?*

Just as Anaïs had helped me work myself out of the Miller forest, so Henry now helped me on her film once we started editing—helped me in his own fashion. Having first challenged me to reach the heights, he now bludgeoned me. Cut that, it's not important! I wanted to use it all, naturally; his own conversation with Anaïs, for instance:

> *and you gave me such great help, because you used to go over my early scripts and say, "Look, don't put that in; it isn't necessary." You used to have to fight me about it because I thought everything was important. Now, you know, if I had the power I would reduce everything. I would write the smallest books if I could.*

On the other hand, when we reviewed the dailies of Anaïs's conversation with me at the tea-table which went on and on, Henry was delighted: "Beautiful, don't cut a frame of it!" But, however beautifully it played uncut, it was much too long, and I made some noticeable cuts. A month or so later, when we reviewed a rough assembly of the film, he exploded, "Dammit, you've cut that and that from the tea-table sequence!" And yet he'd fought me tooth and nail to cut chunks out of the marvelous swimming-pool sequence in his odyssey on the grounds that the audience would get water-logged.

And so it went, week in, week out. And more serious problems surfaced. When you edit film in a small editing room on a moviola with a small picture viewer, you simply can't predict how the film will look on a screen, small or large. So you project the workprint in a viewing room from time to time. But you can't tell how an optical effect—whether superimposition, dissolve, fade-in or fade-out, or even a plain, ordinary cut from one shot to another will play, until the first trial print has been struck from the original negative. (N.B. also called, an answer print. Why? Because it's a question until it's answered.) In the sequence at that tea-table, Anaïs finished a thought, a paragraph, and gazed off into the distance. And then back to me at the camera as she started another thought. Looking at the pause, it seemed much too long. So we cut a few feet out of the film and dissolved to cover the elision. At a sneak preview at UCLA, a professional colleague and friend, well-disposed to positive criticism, said she loved the film, but noted that pause as being too long, as though Anaïs were waiting for a director's or prompter's cue. So I trimmed the pause by a couple of feet more. Then I showed the film to a class I was giving at the time for UCLA Extension. There, one advanced student remarked on that very pause, saying you could almost hear her heartbeat. That was that; I put back the "couple of more feet," plus.

In a conversation with Larry Durrell about time, he said that reality is now 24-frames-per-second, and referred to Cocteau's response to a question about the difference between a photograph of Nôtre Dame, say, and a motion picture film of the same scene: the camera is photographing the passage of time.

Essentially, the moviola has a crude sound system. As with the image, so with the soundtrack. One re-records, mixes the different pieces of sound in order to equalize the varying levels of volume and atmospheres (room tone) of the different filming situations. And when you go into the sound studio to mix, you hear sound at the very highest fi, indeed. But, you take so much for granted—as I was to learn to my great misfortune.

At the first public preview of the completed film (an invitational affair at the Theatre Vanguard), the sound of the very critical opening sequence was awful. It had been a warm evening and the air-conditioning unit had been turned on; but somehow the dampening of its hum had not been worked out. We were appalled. Now all of us—the senior crew, Anaïs, and a few professional friends—went into the sound studio. Well, there is was: on that mood-setting opening sequence there was too much freeway noise that had carelessly been picked up by the sound recordist (who was probably so entranced by the subject on his first encounter, as we all were, that he used the wrong mike). It was overwhelming the fragile voice doing a gray, tear-drop "interior monologue."

There was simply no way out but to "loop" the sequence, a customary proce-dure in Hollywood movies with professional actors. On location sequences, all the sound is recorded with all extraneous noise. When the film is in final rough cut, the actor goes into a sound studio and lip-reads to himself on film, post-recording his lines. Tiresome work: the filmed phrase is put on a loop and run through the projector with cue marks, so that he can anticipate the first word, and the actor records the lines to it. Start, read phrase; pause; cue marks; read phrase, ad nauseam *until he has it right. It is like jumping on and off a merry-go-round until you are exactly in phase with the prancing horses. But he or she is a professional, and Anaïs is not; not that kind of professional.*

I went into the studio apprehensively with the loops, and she came prepared to work hard—and did. But it proved hopeless. The lines coming in on the headphones would impede her response, rather than help her. After a couple of hours she was on the verge of exhaustion and tears; moi aussi. *I was more concerned about her nervous exhaustion, since her health was poor then. So I had her read the lines from the script, after she heard them on the headphones, and prayed that within a few retakes she'd get a reasonable approximation of the rhythm and cadence—and we'd have to leave it to the editor to match word for word, stretch pauses, trim others. But there aren't pauses between every word—they flow as phrases more frequently than as words. Robbie Fitzgerald spent a couple of months at it, and we finally let it pass.*

107

Tom Schiller, Bob Snyder's young associate director, recently returned from a trip around the world.

Tom Schiller: I brought you this little book I found in Japan. I love the little Japanese things, the way they wrap them, and the way they present gifts all the time. . . .

I went to a temple and a Zen priest who couldn't speak any English initiated me into the rites of meditation and the lotus position and all that. He had me seated in the lotus position and I could hear him walking behind me with this stick. He put the stick against my back so that it would get my back straight, and then he put it on my shoulder lightly, and then he went whack! right on my shoulder—you know, to bring me enlightenment. But it just hurt my shoulder.

Anaïs: I read about that. I never really took to the idea.

Tom: I didn't either, no. . . . I just visited India about three months ago and I went to the Sri Auribindo Ashram, and I experienced a really fantastic sense of peace and calm and it didn't require any preparation on my part—I

didn't have to learn the liturgy. I could walk in off the street, sit down, and suddenly a sense of tranquillity came over me, such as people must experience after years of discipline. But after I left the Ashram, it dissolved . . . the further away I got, the more I lost that wonderful feeling. I want to know how one taps into it; it's so difficult to find.

Anaïs: I feel we can't gain that Indian or Japanese sense of peace and calm and keep it permanently by adopting another religion . . . because it belongs to them, they created it. So we have to create it for ourselves in our Western world, in Western terms. We have to create a Western sense of serenity, at peace with our Western psyche, a fusion of our conflicts, a resolution of our duality.

Our culture puts great stress on us, it makes divided selves, as R. D. Laing says. It has made us schizophrenic, it has given us conflicting wishes. We are working in a culture that is really the antithesis of what we're seeking.

We have to find our own way to find this serenity which I now feel simply because my different selves are not in conflict anymore. I feel both energy and a sense of serenity.

Since she's always so beautifully gotten together, I talked to her about dress. She used the phrase *an ethical aesthetic* (or was it an *aesthetic ethic*?) for herself as well as for others.

Would you, then, clean your pool in a party dress?

Why not?

And she disappears into her room, reappearing radiant in a white party dress. We grab the cameras and she picks up a long pole and starts to clean the pool. Just as well now as later!

I never thought of costume purely as an act of seduction.
I thought of it as an aesthetic necessity,
an essential to the totality of our lives. . . .

Some people will really believe that I do clean the pool in this party dress
because I have given the impression of giving costume a great deal of importance.
But it is a theatrical and aesthetic importance
and just as much for the the delight of woman's eyes as for man's eyes.

I am a Pisces.
Pisces ruled by Neptune, the planet of illusion.
Pisces is the planet of the actor.
And the design of it is two fishes,
one going upstream and one going downstream . . .
Pisces is very dual; also filled with empathy for others.
It's the sign of compassion.

The film's trajectory seems to have followed her life pattern, starting in gray—in the rain teardrops of her early quest for her father—and ending in the rainbow of joyous self-realization and serenity.

And my own voyage of discovery? The filmed twenty-four-frames-per-second reality of Anaïs Nin. Simply that; and that's more than enough.

114

Whenever I felt I had to choose between two things,
I always ended up taking it all in.
I never wanted to choose one against the other,
but to harmonize and fuse them into one.
Perhaps this comes close to the Chinese concept of yin and yang
which need each other to complete each other.

I like to feel that I have
transcended my destiny.

ABOUT THE AUTHOR

Film-maker, teacher, and lecturer, Robert Snyder has had a distinguished and pioneering career documenting the greats in the creative and performing arts, of which the most recent are Willem de Kooning, Henry Miller, Buckminster Fuller—aptly called Life Encounters—and Anaïs Nin.

Mr. Snyder's films have garnered many awards, starting with *The Titan: The Story of Michelangelo,* for which he received an Academy Award for Best Documentary Feature in 1951; followed by a Diploma of Merit from the Edinburgh Film Festival for *A Visit with Pablo Casals;* Special Award for the Best Folkloric Documentary, Bilbao, the Ciné Golden Eagle for *Bayanihan Philippine Dance Company;* and the coveted Gran Premio Bergamo for *The Hidden World.*

Born in Manhattan and educated at CCNY and Columbia University, he resides in Los Angeles, California, and lectures periodically on the arts and the art of film at universities and museums here and abroad. He is a member of the Directors Guild of America and of the Academy of Motion Picture Arts and Sciences. He is currently working on a full-length TV-film biography, *Pablo Casals: Of Music and Humanity,* for the Casals Centenary.

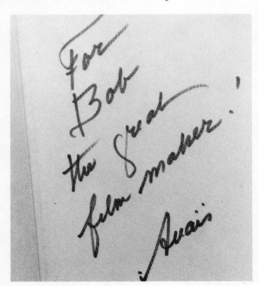

This book was set in
twelve point Aster on Mergenthaler VIP
by Beacon Typesetting, Inc., Panorama City, California,
and printed by
Edwards Brothers, Ann Arbor, Michigan.
The book was edited by Ruth Glushanok,
and designed by Kadi Karist Tint.